In the Midst

PRAYING WITH POETRY

May these poems
bless you,
Renée Hilton-Taylor

RENÉE HILTON-TAYLOR

This is a work of nonfiction.

Ordering Information:

BookTrail Agency
8838 Sleepy Hollow Rd.
Kansas City, MO 64114

Printed in the United States of America

For all of those who have been a part of my journey,
whose inspiration and encouragement
have made this writing possible.
An identifiable list would encompass yet another book.

Preface

To My Readers:

Welcome to my second book of poetry. My first book, <u>Our Everywhere God, Waking Up to God's Almighty Presence through Poetry</u> was published after my husband's death in 2010. These poems are a continuation of my need to share faith in the God whom I find *in the midst* of life. The inspiration to write has come at different times under different circumstances–the back of a child's kindergarten homework, the New Orleans Jazz Fest, sitting on my front porch, enjoying nature, or during a dark night of the soul.

I confess that content and titles may at times be similar. So goes the mind of the student where diversity and repetition are necessary for the lessons to be learned. I have found that themes that are repeated are essential to my well-being, and, so perhaps, to that of my readers. Poetry written in first person is my attempt to prompt the reader to reflect on his or her own personal experiences and benefit from the similarities.

May these poems act as an invitation for you to grow in your awareness of Emmanuel, God with us, and truly *in our midst*.

So dear readers read on; write in the margins, underline or highlight, respond in your journal. Relax-Receive-Rejoice, Amen!

Renée Hilton-Taylor

Table of Contents

A Writer's Reflection..1

Our Deepest Need..2

Just Call Me Simon...3

Who Says?..5

Good News/Bad News 7

Take My Hand...8

Impressions of the 2008 New Orleans's Jazz Fest 9

The Compost of Our Lives 11

Faith Share..13

Lesson of the Basketball Goal 14

Growing Older...16

Divine Dialects..17

Identify, Don't Compare...18

Mystery of the Internet..19

Contentment in Silence..20

Our Everywhere God 22

Soup Days 24

More Than..26

Be the Change 28

Bring It Along 31

Connection Broken 32

Storm Before the Calm 34

Welcome Home 35

The Rhythm of the Falling Rain............................36

Heavenly Embrace 38

The Labyrinth's Call..39

I Say, "Thank You!" 41

Who are They? 42

It's All About Jesus 43

Unto Dust, a Household Meditation..................... 44

Mary Must Have Her Way 45

An Easter Reflection...46

Good Stewardship 47

God's Design 49

The Teacher Did Appear 51

Graceful Moments 52

The Light Within the Tunnel 53

From Time to Time...54

God's in Charge 56

From Sorrow to Joy 57

Joy Born of Love 58

Healing..59

Peace of the Lord 60

The "O" Word..61

Too Busy..62

We Do..63

The Ways of the World..64

Eucharist, a Call to Action 65

Beauty, a Reflection 66

Surrendered 67

A Divine Spark 68

Widowhood, a Promising Desert 69

The Deeper the Hurt 71

Love's Grand Design 72

If 73

Pink Splashes 74

The Father Recycles 75

Suffer the Children 76

An Invitation to Divine Presence 77

Slow Down 78

Alone with God 80

Empowered to Fly 81

Bi-polar Faith 82

An Alleluia Day 83

Fear of Silence 84

Stuck in Traffic 85

Wonder 86

A Welcomed Path 88

Praising God through Stewardship 89

Sacred Waters 90

Lessons Learned in Widowhood 91

A Cardinal Delight 92

The Power of "Yes" 93

The Divine Plural 94

Cane Fields 95

Encouragement 96

Consolations 97

Kaleidoscope 98

Mary, Mother of Jesus 99

Befriend the Pain 100

A Cotton Candy Sky 101

Sunflower Surprise 102

A Day's Work 103

A Generous Spirit 104

In Heaven 105

A Mantra of "Yes-es" 106

The Way of the Father 107

Iridescent Orange 108

Hope 109

A Grey Night of the Soul 110

There Were No Pews 112

Under the Influence 113

Feelings-the Voice of the Soul 114

Nothing on the Calendar 115

A Paradox of Contradictions 116

Not Alone 117

The Lifeline of Prayer 118

Yield 119

Nature Has Her Way 120

Have You Ever? 121

Jesus Weeps 122

Alleluia! 124

A Goodnight Prayer 125

Evergreens 126

The Spider's Web...127

Humanity Unraveled 128

The Labyrinth Calls, Again................................130

Behind and Before 131

The Return of Silence 132

When Faith Becomes Personal 133

Unlimited..134

Roll Back the Stone 135

The Other Side of Darkness...............................136

Original Goodness of God 137

As Near As 138

Alone-ness...139

Prisons 140

Paschal Mystery..141

A Wakeup Call...142

Coffee with Jesus 143

Remember When 144

Vanity..145

Midway In-between 146

The Ugly Battlefield 147

The Field Hospital...148

Moments of Grace 149

Original Love 150

Thy Kingdom Come 151

Stress.. 152

Saints Among Us... 153

The Face of God 154

Heads Bowed 155

Trapped But Not Forgotten... 156

Miracles... 157

Unless... 158

What's Your It?... 159

Holy Nudges 160

Courtship Feeding 161

A Mother's Prayer 162

The Walk.. 163

Jesus, the Way-the Truth-the Life 164

Limitless Love.. 165

Called to Prayer.. 166

Listen 167

From Major to Minor 168

Just About Money 169

Out of Grace 170

Amen and Amen! 171

A Writer's Reflection

With every stroke of pen,
I join the Creator's world
of untold companions
whose eyes have been opened
at the deep level of heart and soul
I see—I hear—I must respond
to keep my spirit alive
A tiny spark fanned by my willingness
a flame appears and burns
Its life and vigor known only by the Great Spirit
who holds the course of its dream
A great flame needs only a spark
aided by an agreeable breath
to become all it could be
One flame unites to another
A great energy makes way for life
to emerge in greater and greater possibilities
The fire of creation
inspires humankind
Life arises from the ashes!

Our Deepest Need

Our deepest need is God
knowing that in our humanness
we have a tendency to go astray.

Like the sheep that wanders off
away from the sound of the Shepherd's voice,
we need a loving faithful rescue
when we make a wrong and harmful choice.

Deep in the soul of all of us
is an indescribably gracious place,
where God has chosen to be intimate
until we see Him face to face.

Just Call Me Simon

As I walk along my way,
others will cross my path
needing a hand to trust and pray.

It is very difficult
if not impossible you see—
to travel life's path in faith
without another to become a *we*.

Jesus had a Simon
as His strength failed the cross—
a Simon who walked beside Him
when it seemed that all was loss.

Our role as followers
of this Divine Brother and Lord
is to be Simons for one another—
Peace and Joy is our promised reward.

So, when others come and want to share
their troubled and broken hearts,
I remember the Simon of Jesus
and open my heart to the listening art.

When my own burdens
are much too heavy to bear,
I will welcome another Simon
who offers the gift of God's loving care.

What a gift the Simons are—
they reflect God's amazing grace
to never leave us unattended,
God so loved our human race.

Who Says?

Who says how our bodies should look
from the top of our heads
to the ends of our toes—
and all the places in between?

Who says what our families should look like
promoting its size? two children will do?

Who says what is in style and what is not
disregarding the virtue of modesty—
where our bodies are held in self-respect
not in shame but in high esteem?

Who says what is of importance
in developing and maintaining relationships—
those intimate connections that hold infinite possibilities
for love to be shared and humankind transformed?

Who says that happiness is an outside job
dependent on acquiring status and material possessions,
rather than an inside gift
dependent only on our willingness to receive?

Who or what is the guide
that directs our thoughts, feelings, and actions?
Who or what is the source
and ultimate goal of our human life?

The answer to these questions
is made visible in the many choices
that make our daily lives a debilitating prison
or an experience of unimaginable freedom.

Good News/Bad News

When our minds become shrouded
with man's inhumanity to man,
our lives become void and uncertain
of the dreams and hopes of God's divine plan.

I'm not one to hide my head in the sand
and look sheepishly the other way,
but too much bad news leaves me feeling hopeless
except for the desire to humbly pray:

"Lord God present in all of your creation,
especially in the hearts of women and men,
may our spirits receive your good news
filled with promises of peace and joy. Amen and Amen. "

Take My Hand

Come and take my hand;
come and walk by my side
for I love you my child
as a groom loves his bride.

Come and take my hand;
come and walk with me
for we're on our way
to a blissful eternity.

Come and take my hand;
oh, do not be afraid,
for I am your Lord
by my life and death you were saved.

Come and take my hand;
come and walk by my side
we'll share a life together
in you I shall abide.

Impressions of the 2008 New Orleans's Jazz Fest

Squish and ooze, squish and ooze—
the rain and dark earth created such muck.
The grassy fields failing to camouflage
the rain soaked ground below.

Yet, the evidence was clear
on feet, toes, shins, knees, faces and hair
and the clothes that clung in between—
festival revelers were committed to having fun!

Rain and lightning made a disturbing visit
torrential waters poured from the sky-
tents were closed, their sides let down
to keep their artists' ware safe inside.

Those who chose to escape the rain
crowded inside sitting where they could
musicians playing with accordion and fiddle
competing with the downpour on the tent high above.

So they sat– eventually in the mud
hair dripping, clothes becoming a second skin
feeling no pain as they "rolled on the river"
an old tune serendipitous for the day.

The rain stopped its interfering ways
inviting humanity to seek for more
tents reopened and the beat went on
there was time left before the fest shut down.

Bands played, the bass vibrating in your chest–
crowds remained hypnotized standing close knit,
unaware and surely uncaring of the time
overwhelmed by the rhythms of the day.

There were no "clean" people here anymore–
too much earth and rain
walking, talking, eating, dancing, buying–
sunburned shoulders, faces red, raincoats parting
hurrying to the next event–differences dissolving
by the movement of the Spirit of this great event!

The Compost of Our Lives

If you've ever had a compost heap
to help your garden grow,
then you know the worth of all things
that into the compost you would throw.

The banana peels and coffee grounds
break down providing richness for the soil,
and when added to the garden
vegetables grow with much less toil.

Our lives are very much the same–
the things we regret and need to throw away
are the very things God can use
when we've wandered and gone astray.

For nothing in our lives is lost
if we allow God's penetrating heat
to transform those sins of ours
as we surrender them into our soul's compost heap.

God takes all those regretful things
and mixes them with our tears of remorse–
transforming those memories from the past
into an energy that becomes a life giving source.

All of life really does matter–
there is nothing God can't redeem.
Guilt and shame belong in our soul's compost
where God's love and mercy reign supreme.

Faith Share

So much of our faith
is based on our personal story–
the bottom line is to trust
in God's all-knowing glory.

He knows our thoughts and feelings
which are rooted deep within,
and He patiently guides us into His Light
away from judgment and sin.

For sin is a turning away
from God's sustaining light–
a light that takes the form of Wisdom
which causes our errors to take flight.

So, let us pray as we journey ahead
united in love for one another
that God's Holy Spirit will lead us
despite differences we share with our brother.

Lesson of the Basketball Goal

The ever so tall basketball goal
stood stately off to the side.
Its backboard had been shattered
surely wounding its competitive pride.

Another new goal stood not too far away–
it looked very much the same,
the only difference it seems
is that its backboard showed no shame.

The two goals caught my eye
as I drove by in my car.
A little fixin' would surely make one ready
for the next great basketball star.

How quick we are in this culture of ours
to replace what's broken with something new.
Instead of fixing our worldly treasures
we thoughtlessly discard—"It's the thing to do!"

But I know what most would say
about my thoughts to wisely conserve–
"It's so much easier to buy another",
instant gratification is what we deserve.

The effects of consumerism in our modern age
should cause us to considerately slow down.
If we continue to gobble up our resources,
in predictable waste we will surely drown.

"Waste not, want not" used to be the creed
that guided our mortal way.
Perhaps we need to revisit its wisdom
and do so without much delay.

Growing Older

Different things matter
now that I am growing older–
It is the simple quieter things that bring peace
and a spirit somewhat bolder.

The dust may sit awhile longer
in the corner of the floor,
but relishing a time for reflection
is a much more consoling chore.

It actually feels wonderfully good
to replace *do*-ing with *be*-ing.
Now in an aging freedom
it is more often my choosing.

I no longer have to hide
behind a shadow of perfection–
I can accept life on life's terms
accompanied by God's ever present affection.

Divine Dialects

God's Holy Spirit speaks throughout our world
in dialects of every imaginable kind—
stirring within the human heart
bestowing insight to souls living blind.

It is truly amazing to think
that God loves us one and all—
destined for the very same kingdom
guided by His Spirit since the first fall.

My prayers come in English
a dialect that I understand,
but the Spirit moves beyond my heart
inspiring the hearts of others in every land.

The dialect of the Spirit
is as diverse as Nature you see—
reflecting God's passionate desire
to converse with you and me.

So, when you are in your prayerful mood
and you hear God speaking to you,
join your heart in holy communion with others
who hear God's voice in a dialect different, yet true.

Identify, Don't Compare

When I see the heavy burdens
that my fellow companions do bear,
I see my own burdens as light
when I reflect, not to compare.

The pain and suffering of loss
no matter how it may show up,
challenges the faithful traveler
to let God fill their life's cup.

To some the loss is so very tragic—
cancer has taken the woman's face
while another's child loses a limb
their courage is gift—God's amazing grace.

I know we are not supposed to compare—
our lives are meant to uniquely unfold
never encompassing more than we can handle
as long as it's the Father's hand that we hold.

And when I see the strength in others
as they bear their heavy load,
their example of acceptance through faith
inspires my heart ten thousand fold.

Mystery of the Internet

The internet is a mystery
I surely don't understand–
so much information available
by just the flick of my hand.

Man has truly fashioned
a gracious piece of art,
with its ability to unite us
or divide and keep us apart.

All things are created for God's glory
to help us on our intended way,
but our free will can misguide us
from God's purpose we're led astray.

So, Praise God from whom all blessings flow
including this marvel of our time.
May we use it for good and God's glory
then through it our light will shine!

Contentment in Silence

There's a certain gracious space
where noise is no longer a distraction—
it is called Silence.

Silence is a gifted response to the ceaseless
chatter and buzz of our busy world
as it collides and bustles about,
always seeking, seeking, seeking—
more, and more, and more.

Silence is where listening
through the ears of the human heart
takes precedence over our obsessive need for *knowing*—
where in an intimate embrace we are free to truly hear
and find peace in *not knowing*.

Silence is the cutting edge
that separates the human heart
from the counterfeit promises of a secular world
and offers the life sustaining gifts of hope and joy.

Once transported to this sacred place
our hearts become transformed
by God's generosity and unearned grace.

So, embrace the gift of silent contemplation;
be rescued from the restlessness of the present age;
enter the presence of our Father, Brother, Companion;
welcome silence, our faithful friend.

Our Everywhere God

How can that be?
In the cancer wards
where there is much pain,
a nurse enters to minister with hope
for the victim his health to regain.

On the battle field of war
where soldiers are torn apart and often die,
a chaplain makes his way offering prayers—
not alone does the victim lie.

On the city streets fraught with danger
where the homeless wander around,
a worker from a sheltered place
offers refuge where safety can be found.

At the kitchen table
where tears are freely shed,
a friend offers a listening ear
praying by the Spirit to be led.

Can there be any place
where our God cannot be?
Is there anything in this life
that can keep us bound and not free?

It is only our unwillingness to respond "Yes"
to God's persistent call:
*Love one another through service
brothers, sisters, even your enemies one and all.
Feed me; clothe me; quench my thirst; comfort me in illness;
visit me in prison; welcome me a
stranger; provide me a bed;
see me in the least of your brethren
and into my heart you will be led.*

Yes! God can be found everywhere
even in the midst of violence and destruction.
We must be God's hands, feet, and heart–
that is His most passionate instruction.

Soup Days

What do you do
when the weather gets grey,
when your mood is somber
resisting even the time to pray?

What do you do
when the future is not clear;
when through distance, busyness, or death
no one is near?

What do you do
when the mood within
is motivated by self-pity–
such a useless ungrateful sin?

What do you do
when no plan is attractive–
when the absence of a solution
holds you hopelessly captive?

Well, I make soup!

I take out the onions and the celery
and sauté them in my cast iron pot.
I add vegetables from my garden–
beans, tomatoes, and broccoli–such a blessed lot.

I keep a vigilant watch
careful to stir and taste
adding broth and seasoning well–
this culinary art is not to waste.

Like the soup that blends all things
to produce a savory dish,
I find my mood does lighten
creating peace, my heartfelt wish.

So when your days do darken
and its light turns to shades of grey,
get to your kitchen and prepare a soup–
its creation is a way to pray!

More Than

We are so much more than
whatever it is that we do,
although from our infant days
achieving success was ours to pursue.

As we began to walk and talk
hands clapped and smiles did abound
encouraging our quest for approval and praise–
no greater pleasure could be found.

On and on throughout our life
we continue to relish success
until some unexpected failure
brings us to our knees in tears of distress.

All the years of *do*ing and accumulating things
no longer brings the happiness that we expected–
we are left with an anxious empty feeling
for our need for *be*ing has been neglected.

Our talents have carried us to levels of success–
we've learned as a student; taught as a teacher.
Now the wisdom of age is teaching us
be-ing not *do*-ing is a journey much richer.

Despite the losses that age does bring
as possessions of all kinds disappear–
we find ourselves in the loving embrace
of our God who holds us so very near.

Gone are the external consolations
of the world of accomplishing things–
space is made in our Sacred Center
for the Joy that comes with simply *be*-ing.

Be the Change

If we are to change
the world in which we live,
we must start with ourselves—
as individuals we have so very much to give.

Social change is all around us
if we have the awareness to see—
humanity reaching out to humanity
in ways that invite you and me.

It may not make the headlines
or be on the nightly news,
but the power of creation continues
to color our world with unbelievable hues.

The water has reached the roof tops
people are stranded everywhere—
boats appear with heroes at their helm,
their mission to rescue shows they care.

The children are hungry,
a house has burned to the ground—
the homeless shelter is open
for necessities to be found.

People are dying from all kinds of disease
so far away in an impoverished land–
doctors and nurses come to their aid
offering time and ability as a helping hand.

The elderly woman needs some assistance
as she tries to slowly make her way
when "May I help you" brings a grateful smile
and transforms the solitude of her day.

Sometimes we get stuck
neglecting this work of human transformation–
our greed, selfishness, and pride infiltrate
and threaten the founding values of our nation.

If change is forced or driven by hatred and fear
the result is not a lasting peace
for it imprisons the defenseless–
justice rises demanding their release.

What do we do when our country is polarized
by the distance between the rich and the poor?
Perhaps the answer lies in *who* it is
that is knocking on our heart's closed door.

We've really had the answer to redemptive change
for more than two thousand years–
it came in the person of Jesus Christ,
whose message was rejected by curses and jeers.

Treating others (to include our enemies)
as we would like to be treated
was his golden rule, the place for change to start–
this message turns our world upside down
for it requires a radical change of heart.

Loving our enemy, forgiving seventy times seven
is not something that we easily do–
none of us follows Him perfectly,
remaining faithful not successful is our goal to pursue.

This answer might seem very naive and overly trite–
much too simple for the contemporary mind
but when we decide to follow His message,
Peace on earth we will undoubtedly find.

Bring It Along

"All that burdens your heart,
bring them along," I say.
I'll help you carry the load–
there are no excuses for delay."

"Bring the unknown, the anxieties and fears,
I don't require you to be burden free.
No indeed! It's your very crosses
that require your humble reliance on Me."

"So bring your procrastination
and all else that holds you back–
I welcome the opportunity to show you
that in my loving presence there is no lack."

"We'll travel this road together–
don't worry about what's ahead.
Stay with me in the present moment–
by my light and wisdom you will be led. "
Love, Jesus

Connection Broken

We're losing the bonds
that hold us together–
a voice, a gaze, a touch,
a hand written letter.

What does the future hold
when as a people we progress,
no longer needing the human touch
settling for less and less.

Leave a message, text, or email–
snail mail is much too slow.
"I don't have the time to write,"
quick and faster is the way to go.

What will the future hold
as we let go of the personal touch–
the book to hold, the letter to enjoy and store.
Oh, I'm afraid we're losing much too much.

Technology offers us many new possibilities
in the area of communication,
but I fear its overwhelming presence
leaves a void in human relations.

It's the tone of voice, the look in the eye,
the physical touch, the letter reread,
the handmade card that's treasured–
their loss is a foreseeable dread.

These are the riches that keep intimacy alive
perhaps to be buried by this present age,
only to be found again in a latter generation
by a disgruntled, yet wisely inspired sage.

For believe it or not
we need the human touch,
and gadgets and air waves
can only do so much.

The pendulum of history does swing
from one pole to the other–
technology never replacing our need
to be fully connected to our sisters and brothers.

So, as I complete these thoughts of mine
typing them into my document file–
keeping a hard copy readily available
relishing its presence with a heartfelt smile.

Storm Before the Calm

I bet you think that I've got it wrong
with the storm before the calm.
but, this title fits my life better–
pain has come before the soothing balm.

I best not cling to the calms in my life,
they are not permanent on this earthly plane
but offer a glimpse of the promised reward
for weathering the storms that come on *land*.

The *land of my life* stretches out so very far
vulnerable to all kinds of storms–
each bringing lessons for me to learn
causing me much anxiety and alarm.

As these storms approach my life
and threaten to destroy the *land*,
the only protection that I have found
is to hold on to my Savior's hand.

So, it is the calm that I seek
but not before storms come ashore.
One day in Eternity I'll live my life in peace
where calm will reign forever more.

Welcome Home

Home is where the heart is—
the heart meaning a place of love.
It can be just about anywhere
that love resides, a grace from above.

Our hearts are made *by* Love *for* love—
if our Creator is to have his way.
In fact, our hearts become discontent and restless
when we resist Love's call, "Be still and pray."

Home used to be a very small limited place
where only a select number could abide.
but now through experience I've learned,
Jesus welcomes us all with arms open wide.

Come all you who are burdened;
come all you saints and sinners, too.
My home is your home and is waiting—
a room is prepared just for you!

The Rhythm of the Falling Rain

I sit on my porch and listen to the rain
as it falls upon the metal roof of my home–
creating with its unsteady rhythm
a natural melody playing for me alone.

Its presence which was predicted last evening
on the weather segment of the news
brings calm and confidence to my dawning day,
chasing away any remnants of the blues.

The dark of the night is slowly fading
and is replaced by shades of blue
announcing the sun rising in the eastern sky–
I am blessed with such a spectacular view.

The trees heavy with rain
Drip their surplus on the grass below
creating a carpet that glistens
as the street light shares its glow.

Once again for the umpteenth time
nature is playing her hand–
providing for all things growing
throughout this glorious land.

Oh, to be so blessed sitting with coffee in hand
protected by my porch's extended roof.
I listen and enjoy God's presence–
the rhythm of the rain, His abiding proof.

Heavenly Embrace

Earthly arms are not meant
to last forever—
only meant to be a comfort
for an undetermined while.

If we depend on the arms of another,
we will find the emptiness
very hard to bear
when they are no longer present.

It is the arms of Jesus, our Brother,
that uphold and comfort us on our way.
His strength is our strength—
let go into His tender embrace.

The Labyrinth's Call

The Labyrinth called,
I walked its path.
The cool May morning
welcomed me;
The whisper of a breeze
caressed my face.
I anticipated blessings.

There are always blessings
when I let go and let God–
One step at a time
Relax, Receive, Rejoice!
The path lay ahead
clearly visible as carefully laid bricks
provided an outline for the way–
all I had to do was follow.

At first the path was easy to see,
then the bricks seemed to disappear.
Oak leaves had fallen and covered the path–
I could no longer see my way.
Had I ventured too far to the right,
or too far to the left?

I could see just a few feet ahead
where the path became clear again
safer, more predictable.
So, I continued walking and trusting
that my feet were carrying me forward
on the path I had begun.

As I continued, I stepped over a fallen branch,
avoided poison ivy, and a fire ant's sting.
Several times I had to stop
and pay closer attention as the path
became buried beneath the earth again.

My journey to the center was complete–
a solitary bench offered a space to rest a while.
I sat with open hands,
"Let me just *be*, Lord....Let me just *be*."
Relax and Receive.

Now as I sit and reflect
I receive its final blessing–Rejoice!
My soul is calm and filled with peaceful joy.
As my steps unwind this favored journey
I am grateful.
I take the blessings of the labyrinth
with me wherever I go this day.....

I Say, "Thank You!"

As the street lights dim and cease to glow
and the sun creeps into view,
I say, "Thank You!"

As the dark of night gives way
to greys and then different shades of blue,
I say, "Thank You!"

As the birds compete with the noise of traffic
singing their songs with unseen partners,
I say, "Thank you!"

As the written prayers of others
inspire my wakening heart,
I say, "Thank you!"

As the early morning coolness
welcomes the anticipated season of Fall,
I say, "Thank you!"

As my heart recites my favored morning offering,
"Thank you God for this day and all that it will bring",
I say, "Thank you!"

Who are They?

Who are they
that judge by worldly standards
projecting their moral values
onto the landscape of the human race?

They judge my belly fat
and count the wrinkles on my face
as if to say that it's physical appearance
that keeps me in God's holy embrace.

Have they forgotten
or, perhaps never knew
that this life is only a passage
leading us to a forever new.

The message to stay forever young
is heralded very loud and clear,
very alluring to my vulnerable mind
tempting the faith I hold so dear.

Jesus never judged by appearances;
He valued the imperfect both young and old–
His message proclaimed a kingdom
where all are welcomed into His eternal fold.

It's All About Jesus

Whether you pray the rosary,
make novenas, pray in tongues, or hum a mantra–
It's all about Jesus.

Whether you stand, sit, kneel,
or prostrate yourself in prayer,
It's all about Jesus.

Whether ordained or lay, married or single,
a member of a religious community, or extended family,
It's all about Jesus.

Whether male or female,
Straight or gay, or of a particular race,
It's all about Jesus.

Whether you keep the Sabbath on day six or day seven,
practice a particular religion, or "None",
the message to *Do unto others as you
would have them do unto you.*
Is all about Jesus.

The Divine took on human form
to heal our fallen nature,
inviting us *all* to receive everlasting life.
That is Jesus!

Unto Dust, a Household Meditation

O Lord God, blessed be the dust!
I find it everywhere–
on top of my tables, in the corners,
beneath every chair.

Blessed be the dust that sits upon the glass
reminding me ever so passively
that this life will not last.

For one day, Lord, in your blessed sight
I'll be dancing for joy at my delight–
no dishes, no laundry, no household chores–
all will be complete in that Land of Yours.

So take heart my sisters who battle with the dust-
learn from its lesson of monotony and disgust.
This world is passing; so do what we can
keeping the vision, a DUSTLESS, Promised Land!
(a young mother's lament written during
my children's pre-school years)

Mary Must Have Her Way

There is a Mary and a Martha in each of us—
our Martha is busy with many things,
while Mary chooses the better portion
and receives the peace that Jesus brings.

The Mary in me must sit a spell
before the Martha has her way.
If I'm not very careful you see,
I'll be doing *my will* without delay.

Scattered plans vie for my attention—
they fill my unsettled mind
until I breathe the breath of prayer,
no peaceful guidance will I find.

"Don't worry," Jesus promises,
as He invites my Martha to come and sit.
"Your list of chores will get done;
I will even lend a hand to accomplish it!"

So when my Mary and Martha struggle
to have their own self-righteous way,
I make sure that Mary's choice comes first—
sitting at the feet of Jesus before beginning my day.

An Easter Reflection

What has happened to this
Christian holy day?
It has been captured by baskets of chocolate
hidden in purple and green plastic hay.

The holiday has become so commercial
following Christmas in the lead—
buying stuff that fills the baskets,
we lose the message we so desperately need.

It is up to us as Christians
to follow Jesus' Way;
to celebrate his Life and Resurrection
so as to rejoice on Easter Day!

Good Stewardship

There was a time when
food was never wasted—
the hides and feathers were used
after the game was gratefully tasted.

There was a time when the skins of vegetables
were thrown into a compost to rot
later used to enrich the garden—
a practical purpose we've seemed to have forgot.

There was a time when hems in a skirt
were large in order to be let down;
when britches became "high waters"
and worn with an embarrassing frown.

There was a time when
electricity was very new—
lights would be conserved
needless use was never to do.

Despite our modern marvels
and all the comforts they bring,
let us always remember to be good stewards
of all the wonders of discovered things.

Our ability to discover something new
allows us to participate in God's ongoing creation–
we've progressed beyond our past
and have become a very affluent nation.

Progress we must! It's part of our human nature–
time does not stand idly still.
So as we tread upon our earthly home,
let's do so according to the Creator's will.

God's Design

Beauty has its purpose
as an embodiment of the Divine.
It attracts us by its presence—
in innumerable ways does it shine.

The diverse explosion of creation found in Nature
with its endless expression of colors and intricate plans,
reminds me that the beauty found in Nature
is our Creator's design, not to be confused as man's.

There is beauty and majesty in all our trees;
there is beauty in the clear skies above;
there is beauty in our waters brimming with life—
all created through God's intentional acts of love.

Some beauty is seen
with the aid of the naked eye—
dawn splashes her colors
across the early morning sky.

Vivid hues of pink and orange
combine with differing shades of gray
to speak to the awakening world,
"God is present, not far away!"

So many ways that beauty
makes its presence known—
eyes see, ears hear, fingers feel.
Earth becomes God's divine throne.

The death of a loved one can cause us to question
God's purpose for all created things.
"What's the use of life and beauty if it vanishes?"
leaving our hearts with no song to sing.

This despairing plea is answered—
our hearts open to the Truth that sees more.
The bountiful beauty that surrounds us
is but a foretaste of what God's design has in store.

Yet, as physical beauty does fade
and it most certainly will,
the Beauty within will remind us,
God's presence is with you still!

For peace and serenity have an innate beauty
no matter the circumstances our lives do hold.
Our Inner Beauty shines forth in the darkness—
a beacon of light for others to behold.

So glory to God for Beauty
found all around us *and* deep within.
Beauty is God's generous design—
the place for Joy to begin.

The Teacher Did Appear

So light of foot did the little squirrel perform
as she flew from tree to tree
searching for manna for her day.

I watched in humble awe and abated breath
fearing to interrupt her daring routine–
flying like a trapeze artist from limb to smaller limb
I wondered how they held her weight.

So graceful and free of spirit she appeared to me–
how confident she did make her way
as she scampered on Nature's tightropes
to gather her anticipated supply.

O little squirrel,
you teach me much about trust–
about taking risks in order to survive.
Your life is filled with the daily routine
of searching for and receiving all that you need.

Perhaps at the end of the day
you fall peacefully into the nest of the Father's love
and exhale a simple prayer, "Thank you"–
a lesson for your student to learn.

Graceful Moments

The clouds painted such a flamboyant pink,
unto a sky so blue—
only in our foolishness
do we dare to question, who? or why?

The *who* is God; the *why* is incomprehensible delight
as our Creator with an unseen brush—strokes
paints a masterpiece for our awakening world.

The early morning colors fade in the
competing shades of sunlight
only to reappear in tomorrow's rising dawn—
giving early risers another heavenly performance
that demands a never ending encore.

Woe to those who sleep away
this time of magnificent presence—
it cannot but inspire the soul with amazing grace.

The Light Within the Tunnel

There are many who would say,
"Don't give in to the darkness
that is causing you such discord;
there's a light at the end of this tunnel,
Jesus awaits, our Risen Lord."

When we enter the darkness of pain and despair
as surely most of us mortals will,
just waiting for the light at the *end* of the tunnel
denies the Light who promised to be with us still.

Our crosses won't go away and mysteriously disappear–
the tunnel will seem impossibly long.
But, the abiding Light at the *end* of the tunnel
desires to keep us company as we travel along.

Sometimes we will stumble and fall
as obstacles block our way,
but the Light that accompanies us
is our faithful guide through each delay.

So the next time that you're advised to keep
your eyes focused on the *end* of the road,
remember Jesus is your Constant Companion
always with you to help carry life's load.

From Time to Time

There was a time when
I'd jump out of bed –
the alarm reminding me
there were mouths to be fed.

The chorus of "to-dos"
sang their anxious song
urging me into action
"Hurry–don't take too long!"

There were errands to run,
clothes to wash, bills to pay.
My adrenalin was in over–drive
so as not to delay.

For so many years
I lived my life this way.
I never slowed down enough
to silence the chorus and sit to pray?

Many years have passed
and my retirement years are here.
Early morning sunrise is quite different–
ever so calmer and gratefully dear.

No alarm clock is needed to wake me
from a sometimes restless sleep.
My inner clockwork rouses me—
I have an appointment to keep.

The invitation to pray is issued in the early morning hours,
encouraging me to be grateful for whatever the day may bring.
My God reminds me daily that He wants to guide my way—
to be the One in charge of each and everything.

The "clamor" to meet the needs of others
has long ago passed me by—
living alone during this season of life
offers a call that I cannot deny.

So, I thank you God for all my history
including the busyness of earlier years,
for *everything belongs* by your merciful plan
transforming our lives by relieving our fears.

God's in Charge

When I truly let God be the One in charge
there is a new Voice from deep within.
It sends messages of love and care
making life better than it's ever been.

For where there were worries—
fears and doubts of all kind,
there now lives a Spirit Guide
whose love is all knowing and sublime.

We humans were not created
to be the ones in charge,
to carry the world on our shoulders—
life's challenges are much too large.

In the Sacred Word to us
and in Wisdom all around
we're told to live our lives in trust—
no greater way to be found.

"I don't take over and force my will
with no regard for your own.
Rather, I wait for you to surrender—
no greater love can be shown."

"Let go, let me be the One in charge
of your life's daily plan.
I alone know the joy in store
when you give me your surrendered hand."

From Sorrow to Joy

Lord God, turn my tears
into a sacred "Yes"–
the sorrow they reveal
is only my human unrest.

The tears they come
from deep within my heart–
my soul mate has moved on
leaving me feeling painfully apart.

But your promise, Lord, of Love Eternal
sets my heart hopeful and free–
reminding me that Marc, and so many others
are waiting for a grand reunion in a blissful Eternity.

Joy Born of Love

When the wound of my grief heals
and the scar of sadness fades away
only on occasion to reappear,
I will find a Joy shared with my loved ones
on the other side of the grave;
a Joy beyond human origin; a Joy born of Love;
a Joy that walks with Hope–
that heals a broken heart.

Healing

How we do want
our bodies, minds, and hearts to heal
quickly, overnight, yesterday, instantly–
we don't like the way we feel!

Patience is the needed virtue
not too common in our world today–
waiting for life to take its course
is censored with "Now, no delay!"

Pain is a Divine healer;
as humans we can't avoid it.
Yet, it's not to be hopelessly clung to–
God desires our good and knows our limit.

Peace of the Lord

"My peace I give to you;
receive it as an unearned grace.
My peace will guide you always
no matter where your place.

My peace accompanies all who ask
as they struggle through life's pain—
prison cells, hospital rooms, homeless shelters,
My peace abides there just the same.

So let my peace be with you—
let it be your constant friend.
It attracts non-believers
who seek the same grace...Amen!

The "O" Word

As we mature in our faith
ever more loyal to the Voice within,
we seek and receive God's Presence
out of love, not fear of sin.

The Father calls us lovingly
to come and be with Him.
His ardent longing speaks to our hearts—
it's a grace from deep within.

Love must live in freedom
if it is to be love at all.
Obligation promotes fear and guilt—
strange bedfellows to the Father's call.

God's love is like a great magnet
that draws us to our Savior's side.
It overcomes our doubts and fears
allowing fertile ground for Love to abide.

So, as we live as Christians
and shine God's light for all to see,
Guilt and fear will vanish—
no need for obligations to even be.

Too Busy

Too busy to watch as the hummingbird
flits from flower to flower;
too busy to begin our day with prayer;
too busy to relax and calm the storm within;
too busy to notice the sunrise as it paints the morning sky;
too busy to rejoice in a new day just begun.
Yet, the Creator of all things does
patiently wait for our attention–
He is never too busy.

We Do

God doesn't see the "fat",
we do;
God doesn't see the wrinkles,
we do;
God doesn't see the deformities,
we do;
God doesn't judge by outward appearance,
we do.
God only sees the Spirit Life within;
we can too.
Lord, may looking good by our modern
standards be surpassed by loving
acceptance of Your standards, for Your honor
and glory and the transformation
of humankind. Amen.

The Ways of the World

What we have learned
and what we are teaching
gives rise to a generation
which is constantly reaching.

Reaching for more and more–
no satisfaction or gratitude found.
The world's resources squandered–
injustice, destruction, and poverty abound.

Yet, Jesus was born into this very world,
the Father's gift to us all.
The world became His home for a while,
inviting humankind to answer His call.

But we humans have an independent streak
living life in self-will run wild–
heedlessly striving to satisfy our desires
trampling on the needs of the future's child.

So, let us live at a slower pace
reverencing life as it is meant to be–
living with due respect for our world
insures the Creator's gifts to you and me.

Eucharist, a Call to Action

We receive with a humble response, "Amen"
then action is required on our part—
fostering a spirit of unity
through service from heart to heart.

Jesus lives in every marcel of bread
blessed by his holy name—
when received in the Spirit of faith,
our lives are renewed—no longer the same.

Transformed from our old self-centered ways
like the wineskins of old,
our hearts become more serviceable—
willing to minister in the Shepherd's fold.

Do not resist the invitation to come and receive—
the Father's Kingdom is truly within our reach.
It is found in acts of love and kindness—
that is the action the Eucharist does teach.

Beauty, a Reflection

The calling card of nature beckons us to pay attention–
God is all around!
In vibrant shades of color in trees, flowers, and sky;
in intricate varieties of animal life both large and small;
in elaborate shapes of all things
fashioned by the Creator's hand;
in the revolving cycle of life with its endings and beginnings;
in the unique designs of the human person–
all give certitude to Creation's power
to stir the Unseen within,
if only we practiced respect in guarded stewardship.

And, *there is always more*–
continuous discoveries found in creation
quicken our enthusiasm
as we encounter yet another profound reality
when we thought our knowledge was complete.

"I'm here; I'm here; I'm everywhere–
even as your rapid pace imprints creation
with destruction and waste;
even as your physical beauty fades
and inner beauty is ignored;
even when your love for enlightenment neglects the Divine;
even, even, even–my beauty will prevail.
It is my very nature; it is my gift; it is my Eternity."

Surrendered

The clouds sail across the southern sky
not a sound do they make.

The bird's wake-up call interrupts the early morning silence
accompanied by the drone of early morning traffic—
speeding cars, trucks, and buses all making their way
to meet the demands of yet another day.

The clouds appear single-minded as
they glide along with ease—
so surrendered to the winds of a predetermined destiny.
My imagination wonders in captivated awe:
where have they been, and where are they going?

The dark shades of grey predict
a rain storm looms ahead—
not always a welcomed fate
but needed just the same.

And when their work is done—
no more rain to shower upon the earth
clear skies will reappear,
the reward of dying to self.

Oh, that I could live in such surrendered freedom—
relinquishing my own self-deluded will
trusting in the Great Unseen,
who knows where I have been, and where I am going.
Aaaaah, the essence of faith!

A Divine Spark

There is a Divine spark within our very heart—
the breath of the Spirit waits to set it aflame
and when it catches and begins to blaze,
we are transformed—never the same.

Our world takes on a new meaning—
God's will is our one desire.
The tiny spark of Divine Love
becomes an all-consuming forest fire.

Forest fires cause a lot of destruction
as they burn in Nature's way,
for its pruning work makes possible
for new growth to display.

Don't be afraid of the fire within
of the pain and damage it will cause—
our nature, like the great forest,
needs to embrace the resulting pause.

So, let the gentle Spirit blow—
a nudging breath at the very start.
Let the spark become a great flame
heralding new life from within your heart.

Widowhood, a Promising Desert

Being a widow can seem such an empty place—
gone is the physical presence to sit by my side
to talk, laugh, and cry, and just *be* with—
in another place does he now reside.

Widowhood is much like a desert,
at least in the beginning you see.
All appears desolate and lifeless—
nothing growing to fill the void—just me.

In granted time the rain of tears
water the seemingly barren ground,
and little by little life before unseen
breaks forth and new beginnings abound.

As I journey this unfamiliar path,
I seek the hand of Acceptance with Joy
to help me embrace this new adventure
where fears and doubts my peace cannot destroy.

This *new normal* which graciously does appear
is not foreseen by my own anxious mind,
but is planned for my ultimate good
by my Divine Companion, generous and kind.

So, I will remain grateful for this desert,
Faith tells me there are gifts yet to come—
a life of amazing new beginnings will appear
as I follow in acceptance, "Thy will be done."

The Deeper the Hurt

Hurt can slash a wound within our very hearts
where resentment can have its way,
leading us down a most treacherous path–
no peace to be found throughout our day.

Holding onto, or denying these painful hurts
that are part of our painful past
only keeps us chasing after rainbows
whose promises of relief do not last.

When we embrace the wounds of the heart
and make room for Love to reside,
we enter a humble peaceful place
where forgiveness heals our self-centered pride.

It is the Father's most merciful plan
to use the hurts that cause us such pain
as opportunities to forgive those who have injured us–
Peace and Serenity being the graces to gain.

Love's Grand Design

Love is—
As diverse as the color that surrounds us
with shades that capture the human eye;
As diverse as the animal kingdom both large and small
who share our inheritance, Mother Earth;
As diverse as the quality of humankind
wth its incredible sizes, shapes, and colorful hues
showing no favor;
As diverse as the plant life that springs
forth from the crust of the earth
and offers nourishment to the body
and joyful appreciation to the noticing eye;
As diverse as the words that try to capture Love's essence
only to bow to an inadequate expression;
As diverse as the promising acts of kindness
that applaud the power to forgive.
Love's design expands our human limitations:
to embrace the diversity that surrounds us;
to reduce the self and magnify the other;
to welcome the unity which is meant to be.
What a Grand Design!

If

If our existence is measured only in present time
with no vision of the *everlasting*;
If the value of suffering is denied
and replaced by fleeting pleasures;
If discovery is lost to the quest of instant gratification
and stewardship loses its vital importance;
If time becomes filled with a relentless busyness
and peace of mind is lost to the spirit of chaos;
If forgiveness is replaced by the justification of revenge
and war becomes our primary option;
If love is reduced to a comfortable feeling
and our enemies are judged and condemned;
If we live as if life ends at death
and forget the promise of the Kingdom;
If we forget the Way of Jesus
and his call to die to self in order to conquer death;
then life on earth becomes our hell.
Yet, if we follow in the footsteps of the Master
and love God and our neighbor as ourselves,
then life on earth will introduce us to his Kingdom
which is now and to come... Amen!

Pink Splashes

Pink, Pink, Pink
splashed all along the roadway—
little buttercup faces smiling upward
some hidden, almost unseen.
Even in the early morning rush
with traffic backed up along the interstate;
Even with the blue light flashing
sending a message of caution for what lies ahead;
Even as the clock on the dash reminds me
that time by its very nature waits for no one;
Even as low hanging clouds
predict to dampen the day;
Even, even, even—
an outrageously gracious God is present
to the eye that cares to see!

The Father Recycles

Nothing in the Father's Great Design
is ever wasted
but drawn into His re-creation
of things unwanted;
Nothing overcomes the Father's power
to transform the hideous into the sublime;
Nothing keeps the Father's love
from crowning suffering with a blessing;
Nothing is beyond His repair
through the mystery of salvation;
Nothing–that is unless
we refuse to embrace the potential of miracle
and keep our human imperfections
buried beneath denial within our hearts;
Then life becomes a vast wasteland
void of limitless possibilities;
Rejoice and trust in the promise of Redemption–
release those hurts flamed by injustice
into the hands of the Great Recycler
where the worst of the worst
becomes the glory of the glorious–
despite death, our Paschal Mystery lives!
Alleluia-Amen

Suffer the Children...

My house is quiet now
although in much disarray—
nothing is where it should be
"Calm my anxiety, Lord" for this I pray.

For much of my feeling secure lies
in having everything in its place
and as I look around my home
my perfection cries out, "What a disgrace!"

There is milk on the table, some splattered on the floor,
blankets and pillows in the most inconvenient places.
the questions and chatter have been replaced—
solitude and silence compete as welcomed graces.

It won't take me long to put my house in order—
this belongs here; that belongs over there
and what in the world are Cheerios doing
dried to the floor beneath my unsuspecting chair!

Yet, the love I have for these grandchildren of mine
far outshines the discomfort of chaos—
and if I let disorder rob my peace
my life would suffer a very great loss.

For as the SUV backs carefully down the drive
its passengers ready to meet the rest of their day,
I hear those precious voices through windows rolled down
chanting in unison, "I love you, Née Née."

An Invitation to Divine Presence

Do you ever wonder
what goes on under ground
as the seed begins new life—
such a great marvel to be found!

The seed is such a small creation
some larger than another,
but all "die" within the earth
to bring forth life like no other.

How can such a small seed
grow into plants, flowers, and trees?
It was only a tiny thing before,
now it's a haven for birds and bees.

Look for the miracles!
Scatter some seeds upon the ground.
Let life burst into view—
the Creator is at work; His glories abound.

Slow Down

If we don't stop moving and be still
we miss so very much–
Nature pulsing with abundant life
reflecting our Creator's awesome touch.

The touch of Nature's presence
can keep our spirits high
reminding us by its splendor
that our God is forever nigh.

As near as the shades of green
that adorn our summer trees;
As near as the changing seasons
that often bring a welcomed breeze.

As near as the spider-lilies
that spring from their Summer rest;
As near as the migrating birds
traveling Nature's path to make their nest.

The plant and animal kingdoms
are all part of God's glorious array–
created in wise synchronicity
each having a role to play.

We, created in the image of God,
are meant to reverence and behold
for it is in partnership with all of creation
that we witness God's Kingdom unfold.

There are no words to fully describe
the wonder and beauty all around.
We must be still and let Nature speak her truth,
"Look here, your God to be found!"

Alone with God

Our inner void is filled
when we're alone with God—
where distractions are kept at bay.

Our inner void is filled
by the power of prayer
inviting our God to companion our day.

Our inner void is filled
as quiet moments allow
for the Voice of Wisdom to be heard.

Our inner void is filled
as our plans disappear into the quiet realm
making way for greater plans still.

Our inner void is filled
when being alone creates a place at our table
for Acceptance with Joy to sit in divine fellowship.

Our inner void is filled
with overwhelming gratitude for the gift—
Alone with God, our Source of Peace.

Empowered to Fly

The bird flew from perch to perch
all along the telephone wire
then soared to unseen places.
My heart flew with her in deep desire
to fly with such freedom and abandon
with blue skies of promise waiting.
Only my doubts and fears hindering me–
an untrusting heart desiring to be free
Spirit of the Living God
empower me to fly this day
receiving your love then giving it
to others I meet along the way

Bi-polar Faith

Sometimes my faith
has me soaring to a great mountaintop
with indescribable peace, joy, and hope–
all those gifts of the Spirit meant
to console a distracted human race.

Sometimes my faith
travels through the dark cellar of despair
forgetting the consolations of the past–
where desolation threatens to extinguish
the Light which has promised constant companionship.

But I make it through the unmarked journey–
the hand of Light being *Oh* so much stronger
than any darkness that threatens to imprison and destroy.
I am rescued; I rest in gratitude–this
dark night has ended. Amen!

An Alleluia Day

Some mornings are just perfect—
the air is cool and filled with traces of fog
lingering in a distant field.
The songs of my feathered friends
echo in the absolute stillness—
their private conversations cloaked in mystery.
From far off I hear the morning wakeup call
of a rooster who welcomes Brother Sun
as he paints shadows across my lawn
and makes his presence known.
These tranquil moments introduce me
to a new day and all that it will bring—
an *alleluia day* to be celebrated and enjoyed
in the Spirit of Gratitude—all is well.

Fear of Silence

I wonder why there is such discomfort
when silence becomes the only *sound*–
fear laments and makes predictable excuses
careless noise has won another round.

Slowing our pace and stilling the mind
is not in the modern's view.
There's too much to accomplish–
our lists are filled with things to do.

In this age of hustle and bustle
with our senses in constant stimulation,
our soul cries out for required relief
from ever-increasing stress and tribulation.

What is it that causes such fear
when silence is brought to mind?
Perhaps it is the *unholy* voice–
"No peace in silence will you find."

"Face those fears," the *Holy* Spirit counters–
"Silence is such a welcoming place
where the folly of a distracted world
is replaced by my amazing grace."

Stuck in Traffic

Cars and trucks big and small
inch along their morning trek
to worlds unknown to me.
I wonder as these strangers-yet-companions
pass me by in a flurry to a focused destination,
what burdens or joys they carry–
for that will make a difference
as they commune with others.
They will shed light or darkness–
the choice made by the god, or God,
whom they choose to serve.

Wonder

The delicate vine twists and turns
clinging to the provided support
later to produce its predictable bean—
the very source from which it began.

I wonder in amazement
at the pin dot of a seed that develops—
its vine inching upward, upward, upward,
its limbs reaching for the sun
as it escapes the womb of the earth to produce
that for which it was destined.

I wonder in frustration
as the carpenter bee burrows its hole—
the wood dust falling like snow
evidence that she has returned
for Spring to have her way.

I wonder at the marvel
of the mole whose burrows mark my yard
as he follows an instinctive roadmap
to find sustenance from the dark and damp earth.

I wonder in gratitude
as the sunflower surprises
an uninvited, yet welcomed, guest–
"Look to the Sun," her voiceless plea.

I wonder with a shade of envy
as the cardinals take flight–
He following she
until they perch–courtship feeding has begun.

I wonder if we foolish moderns
realize how much we miss
of the Creator's gracious touch–
found in the marvels all around.
Cherish the grace to wonder.

A Welcomed Path

The "Y" grass* welcomed me;
the weeds tempted me;
the rocky soil disturbed me;
the path itself calmed me;
the obstacles reminded me;
the bench invited me;
the great oak cooled me;
the tears healed me;
the returned way encouraged me;
the squirrel's diggings delighted me;
the blue flower surprised me;
the poison ivy warned me;
the end of the path challenged me;
The "Y" grass awaited me
and sent me on my way–
Amen and Amen!
(*Refers to *Bahia grass* which grows in warm
climates and whose Y-shaped stem holds its seeds.
The Y-shape invites a *"Yes"* response to life.)

Praising God through Stewardship

We praise God when we
recycle that can;
adjust the thermostat;
conserve water remembering those with none;
wear that shirt just a little longer;
reduce our portions;
do with less which is so much more on a worldwide scale;
reuse, reduce, recycle, renew the face of the earth–
as good stewards for the honor and glory of our Creator;
let it begin with me...

Sacred Waters

The waters of life are there
enveloping the new life just begun–
supporting, comforting, lubricating
as the living being becomes more and more
responsive to its own existence
until the confinement is no longer meant to be–
and the initial waters that cradled the living
burst forth introducing new life–
sacred waters, holy waters
the Rite of Introduction has occurred.

Lessons Learned in Widowhood

The silence in being a widow
has opened the door
to the silence of learning–
empty space offers time to explore.

More time to listen
to really hear
from the Heart of Hearts
that Love is always near.

Loneliness may come
and visit for a while
but, never alone Jesus reminds me–
arms outstretched with an understanding smile.

Now is the time in these twilight years
to embrace this sacred space–
to fill it with an enduring peace
unlimited, unearned amazing grace.

Never doubt the Savior's love
No matter what life does bring,
Be still in the quiet to find
God's presence in each and everything.

A Cardinal Delight

Good morning my Cardinal
where is your mate—
am I disturbing your early morning rendezvous?
You seem not to care
as you pillage for Nature's supply—
you fly beneath this great canopy
of tangled branches that have seen many years.
So much freedom and ease
interrupting my thoughts with a welcomed thrill
the day has begun—
ripples on Cane River* appear and fade;
our feathered brothers and sisters take flight
in this great space of time
All is well—
our Creator smiles.
* in Natchitoches, Louisiana

The Power of "Yes"

The *yes* of Love birthing creation;
The *yes* of redemption
through the Incarnate Jesus;
The *yes* of Mary to surrender her body
to carry our Savior;
The *yes* of death and suffering
to allow victory through resurrection;
The *yes* of the Divine Spirit
to accompany us on our journey
of daily possibilities;
The *yes* of repentance
allowing for healing;
The *yes* of freedom
to choose the holy:
The *yes* of Love
granting mercy and forgiveness;
The power of Love
inviting the Eternal "Yes!"

The Divine Plural

Always united—Three in One
where Love knows no limits;
a relationship we are called to enter;
a Threesome that hounds us
to become one with the Eternal
Father, Son, and Holy Spirit;
the Divine Plural that has known us
before we entered the womb;
the Divine Plural that takes us beyond death
into an anticipated embrace;
One in Spirit—thought, emotion, word, deed
the Divine Plural anxiously awaits our arrival
to proclaim, "All I have is yours!"

Cane Fields

Green, green, ever so green
standing so tall for acres and acres
as far as the eye can see.
The stalks stand victorious
over Nature's random call–
Once flattened by wind beyond its strength to bear.
the earth remained dormant
waiting for a new Spring.
Rejoice! The cane has returned–
it thrives despite the threat.
Will the wind with a name blow once again;
will the stalks become this year's harvest,
or the collateral damage of Nature's fury?
Time will tell.
In the meantime, the teacher has appeared–
Nature has taught her lesson.

Encouragement

Don't worry so
but, I'm only human;
Don't envy your neighbor
but, I'm only human;
Don't lie
but I'm only human;
Don't harbor resentments
but I'm only human;
Don't forget Me
but I'm only human.
I know–
that is why I became human.
Now come; no more excuses.

Consolations

God is with me:
in the song of the bird,
in the color of the zinnia,
in the sunlight of early morning,
in the calm of solitude,
in the peace in my soul,
in the care of family and friends,
in the memories of the past,
in the hope of the future,
in the present moments of now,
in the comfort of my porch,
in the inspiring written word,
in the grace of gratitude.
Amen and Amen!

Kaleidoscope

Like assorted pieces of colorful broken glass
held in creative tension
our world is transformed into intricate patterns
caused by the reflection from mirrors
one human; one Divine–
a child is born – there is no food
the space craft landed – another beheading
bible study tonight
the tigers are endangered
the rhythm of Nature – the Monarchs migrate
the mudslide swallowed the mansion
peacemakers unite in prayer
she has no shoes
obesity is epidemic
Akiane's paintings – collection for the poor
global warming denied
racism provokes violence
food prices rising
doctors without borders
the universe expands – we are all connected
a Pope teaches mercy and inspires the humble.
The kaleidoscope of humanity–
Who can see the pattern? Who can give it meaning?
The answer lies in our hearts
where the God of Unlimited Possibilities intervenes
and turns the cylinder of history–
New worlds appear!

Mary, Mother of Jesus

There was an earlier time when I saw Mary
in beautiful statues crowned with a floral wreath
capturing my childhood imagination.
Her home was orderly and immaculately clean–
her days filled with joy and peace like no other.
There is a time now since I have traveled a mother's way
that I see Mary, the Mother of Jesus
tired, afraid, sorrowful, yet faithful.
There is a time now that I pray to Mary
out of gratitude–
inspired by her example of
surrender, acceptance, and forever faithful.
Now I relate.

Befriend the Pain

For She is a given—
no one goes through life without her presence
staying longer with some than with others—
She finds her way in
even in the best protected homes—
like a thief she robs you
of your most prized possessions—
peace, serenity, hope and joy.
As she enters through a vulnerable place
the wise acknowledge her presence
through the discomfort she brings—
an unholy spirit of discord, restlessness, and discontent.
Denying her presence only prolongs her stay
for she flees at the sound of her name.
We need not go searching for Pain—
she is part of the life we live,
sights we see, sounds we hear, feelings we feel.
She enters through the window of time
to become a source of grace—
for those who choose to embrace her,
thereby soothing her sting.
The courageous never leave Pain alone
to roam the inner chambers of the heart.
Once she is gone the house is quiet—
hindsight speaks; wisdom rejoices
for without Pain there would be
no resulting Peace.

A Cotton Candy Sky

Like cotton candy stretched across
a bright blue sky,
wisps of pink transparent to early morning light
herald in a new day–
Awake! Awake!
Rise from your slumber–
Acceptance with Joy awaits the expectant heart
no fear or worries;
just what is;
always good–
the Candy Maker's promise.

Sunflower Surprise

A sunflower springs from the compost–
Surprise!
An unintended Joy
the seed of its existence
only known by the Great Sower–
a seed smothered in the decay
of human frailty–
a seed declaring victory
as it rises to face the sun
and follow its course across the daytime sky.
The compost dies in order to give life
and startles the doubtful!

A Day's Work

Headlights burn in the early morning haze
slumber begins to rise—
silence is broken.
Like ants in a disturbed mound
programed for survival,
we scurry on our way—
building, re-building, building
until the job is done.
Time takes its toll—
the sun takes its rest
in the western sky.
We return to our *mound*
another day's work complete.

A Generous Spirit

The Spirit of Creation cries out for expression—
no fear; no doubt
Just do it!
Because you can't not
or, you will die—
Paint, sing, write, make love, forgive, dance
Cook, sew, build, plant
experience freedom; discover more
Surprise the world!
The Creator is generous beyond measure.

In Heaven

In heaven
we won't have to count calories
water the lawn
weed the garden
look for a job.
There are no clocks in heaven,
no waiting rooms
or prisons of any kind.
The rivers and oceans are pristine
the air is fresh
the food supply endless.
There are no crosses to bear
no place for fear to hide
no need for forgiveness.
Humanity can project such a limited view
where the unknown is truly unimaginable!

A Mantra of "Yeses"

As my day begins
before my feet hit the floor
I sit on the edge of my bed
and pray to God once more.

"Thank you Father
for all that this day will bring,"
This prayer prayed so often
has become one of my cherished things.

Yes, Yes, Yes
As I begin my day
Yes, Yes, Yes
to all that comes my way.

Hills, valleys, joys, sorrows
and all that lies in between,
no matter the circumstance
I pray "yes" to the Divine Unseen.

"All things work together for good"
for those who follow the Shepherd's Voice.
I am grateful to God Almighty
for helping me make this daily choice.

The Way of the Father

My children:
I allow sickness
in order to send a Physician–
I allow sorrow
in order to send a Comforter–
I allow you to hurt one another
in order to send Forgiveness–
I allow poverty
in order for Generosity to respond–
I allow prisons
in order for Transformation to occur
I allow danger
in order to send an Angel–
I allow injustice
in order for Hope to be born–
I allow lack of faith
in order to send a Savior–
I allow self-will
in order to show Mercy–
I allow fear
in order for my Love to prevail.

Iridescent Orange

Iridescent Orange over Black and White Stripes
draws the tentative glance of people driving by
on their way to *somewhere*.
Do they see or even care that
the iridescent orange over
black and white stripes are there?
Some will judge–
"They are lying in the bed
they have made."
Some will deny their own possibilities–
"Never!"
Walk in their shoes
and your vision will change.
All I could do was pray for
The Iridescent Orange over
Black and White stripes–
fellow prisoners of a different sort.

Hope

Hope is the small patch of blue
that peeks from beneath the
covers of grey–
a welcomed sight for all to behold
and be reminded of the Ever-Present,
even when unseen.
It is when the clouds of grey
camouflage the sky
that Hope is born–
for our memory holds the shades of blue
and the past sheds light on the
presumed present darkness.

A Grey Night of the Soul

I hear the voices that chatter within
stating their needs and woes.
I know they want me to listen to them
occasionally we come to blows.

I'm learning that I, fortified by grace
can listen and not be overcome,
because those voices are only a part of me
not the whole, just a part of the sum.

When I feel fearful as they try to take charge,
I sit and go within.
After they've had their say
I "Let go and let God" in order to begin again.

Sometimes I'm not so sure
about acknowledging these voices within,
but denying their lot and trudging ahead
only increases their control—a fear based sin.

It's quite a challenge to be quiet just to listen,
not to interrupt and direct the show.
Practicing this humble art is a must–
Wisdom says it's how I will grow.

The Seeker in me dares not to sit
and encounter the rumblings from within.
She's impatient with life–always questing for more
Plunging ahead determined this time to win.

So what's on your mind Rebel, Wounded Child, Critic–
all clamoring to have their say.
Patience interrupts and reminds me once more,
"Be stouthearted and wait," Wisdom is on her way.

"O Guide of My Soul–Spark of the Divine,
how grateful I am that you abide within.
You lead me in right paths–
Acceptance, Courage, and Serenity. Amen!"

There Were No Pews

In the beginning there were—
a people seeking a Messiah
crowds seeking justice
blind seeking sight
deaf seeking the spoken word
the lame seeking to walk
sinners seeking forgiveness
In the beginning there were—
roads to be traveled
companions two by two
communities breaking bread
believers sharing their experiences
disciples recognized by their love for one another
In the beginning there was—
standing room only
there were no pews......

Under the Influence

Not under the control of a mood altered behavior,
but *under the influence* of the Life Giving Substance
of God's Holy Grace;
I no longer live in fear of things to come
of maybes and what ifs;
I no longer see the world through anxious eyes,
an unfriendly place;
I cast aside worry and live in the Present Moment,
the NOW being where God awaits to guide me
throughout my day;
I reach out in love freely, spontaneously
without expectations of return;
I begin my day looking forward to successes
both large and small;
I practice patience and tolerance for those people
who annoy me and frustrate my plans;
I pray "Okay God let's live our day together
in Peace and Joy."
I'm at Peace with Myself, My God, and Others.
Thank you Father for the unearned
gift of Your Divine Influence,
an altered state of being!

Feelings—the Voice of the Soul

Deny and become ill—
embrace in the current of courage
find their healing remedy
make room for them all.
Slow down, pause to listen
despite the pain—
Let the soul speak her voice
renouncing the Contemptible Deceit
for hidden beneath that shadow of fear
awaits the Light of Peace and Serenity.
The soul longs to speak—
but succumbs to a fatal existence
as feelings lie scattered on the battlefield of the soul—
their voice no longer heard,
a dreadful silence.
Light is no more......darkness prevails—
yet, another Voice beckons,
"Pour out your heart before the Lord".
Give the soul her voice to sing healing melodies
of Hope, Healing, and Joy. Amen!

Nothing on the Calendar

The little square printed on the month of the year
is empty–
it stands among the crowded scrawls of sister days.
No appointments or obligations absorbing
the minutes and hours of this particular day–
a welcome sight, a delightful reprieve
from the goings and doings of the holidays.
Celebrate–a Savior has been born unto us!
Nothing on the calendar invites
a deeper more profound reflection.

A Paradox of Contradictions

We know so much
and love so little–
knowledge distracting us
from its Divine Source.
We discover the workings of creation
and squander and neglect its care–
we live too fast, too busy
and wonder at our unrest.
Yet, some *do* pray; some *do* see and hear–
the faithful remnant still *does* exist.
The Creator shows the way–
God is sovereign despite our foolishness,
there is always Hope!

Not Alone

When writers write;
dancers dance;
painters paint;
singers sing,
they are not alone.

When birth cries out;
a cure is discovered;
a tear escapes;
Spring buds forth,
we are not alone.

When relationships heal;
night becomes day;
breath continues;
loss is grievous,
we are not alone.

When the Creator creates, comforts, and celebrates
the world is amazed
forgetting the Source of it all.
Humanity in its self-centered folly progresses in hasty fashion
as if it was in center stage and in charge.

When failure appears and disaster seems evident
the Ever Present cries out,
"O humanity wake from your slumber
of too many cares.
Surrender your plans made in isolation—
you are not alone!"

The Lifeline of Prayer

Prayer—
reminding us You are always there
lighting our way through an unfamiliar passage
when life becomes a questionable maze.

Praise You, Father for this gift of prayer—
your call to us to be courageously aware.
Your love covers us and keeps us secure
despite the world's deceptive allure.

I cannot imagine a life void of prayer,
a world of darkness to beware.
There is no need to worry of such a fate—
Jesus is the Victor; the devil is too late!

Yield

The road ends abruptly
choices loom–left or right?
Standing in darkness
a Light advances
showing the way–
the path is before me.
In haste I could proceed
only to allow the darkness
to find me again.
Yield to the Light–
follow, do not lead.
"Be stouthearted and wait on the Lord"
to show you the way!

Nature Has Her Way

The pecan tree self-prunes, or so it seems—
Nature has her way;
branches large and small make it to the ground
in wind and in calm—
Nature has her way;
along with rain and sunshine
the tree reaches tremendous heights,
its fruits falling to the ground—
Nature has her way;
where majesty once stood among the many
a completed journey has fallen—
Nature has had her way.
Our on self-pruning mimics our companions—
"Limbs" lose their strength and fall
into the compost of the awaiting soul.
Endings make way for new beginnings—
Nature has her way.

Have You Ever?

Have you ever looked at a flower,
captivated by its rich color and intricate detail–
or, admired the cardinal with its vivid red color
that catches your eye as it wings across the yard?
Have you ever listened to the melody of the song bird
waking the morning slumber–
or, enjoyed a symphony that both
excites and calms your soul?
Have you ever tasted the natural sweetness of a peach
savoring its flavor, wishing it to remain;
or, relished the reward of a cool drink of water
as it quenches your aching thirst?
Have you ever felt the strength of a heartfelt embrace;
or, the comfort of a warm blanket on a cold winter's night?
Have you ever smelled the scent of the mint growing profusely
in the corner of your yard;
or, the earth wet after the rain has passed?
Have you ever rejoiced in your ability
to experience life through your senses
as an introduction to the Kingdom to come?
Questions invite answers; let us begin!

Jesus Weeps

Jesus weeps as
the hungry are left hungry,
the homeless are left homeless,
the naked are left naked,
the imprisoned die alone.
Jesus weeps when
hate prevails over love,
guns and violence take over our cities,
drugs are the answer,
our brothers and sisters are seen as "aliens".
Jesus weeps when
the unborn child is discarded,
our water and air is polluted,
trash covers our countryside.
Jesus weeps when
we are too busy,
false gods prevail,
we suffer the results of self-induced chaos.
Yet,
Jesus rejoices with the remnant
who seek peace and justice,
who live as His disciples,
who recognize His voice.

Jesus rejoices when
new life is birthed,
Mother Earth and all her inhabitants
are cherished and protected,
sister reaches out to brother desiring their good,
divisions are reconciled,
we see ourselves as related to the Divine.
Weeping and Rejoicing—what shall it be?

Alleluia!

Why save "Alleluia" for Easter?
The alleluia of the Resurrection is forever present–
each *now* moment filled with Divine Presence.
Let us open our minds, hearts, and souls
to be filled with *alleluia* eyes to see
the Love of God that surrounds us in all things! Amen

A Goodnight Prayer

The hours of the day have slipped into the past–
night falls.
Where did God lead you this day?
Did you answer Love's call with a grateful "yes",
I will go; I will follow?
Or, did you go your own way,
Not now; later is a "no"?
Our days are filled with opportunities–
choices abound to bring God's Kingdom into the *now*.
"Lord God, thank you for your graces
to follow you this day; forgive my failings–
help me do better tomorrow. Good night. Amen and Amen"

Evergreens

In the midst of a crowded landscape
the evergreen stood—
a stark contrast to the barren branches
of its neighbors who had lost their vibrant color
to a season past.
Now shades of grey declared a Southern fall.

What a proclamation to the contemplative mind
a mind that sees beyond—
To be in the world and not of the world
To remain ever-faithful and ever-green
despite the Fall/Winter seasons of life
To be a reminder of God's Ever-Presence
regardless of the crowd fencing it in.

The Spider's Web

How does the spider know
to precisely spin her delicate web?
Its threadlike pattern catches my eye—
by the Great Spirit she is led.

For God's Holy Spirit does live
in all created things
each having a gift to share—
a joy to the world its presence brings!

Oh, humanity
do slow down!
See, hear, feel, and savor
the Creator's presence all around.

The song of the bird, the cardinal's vibrant coat,
the blooms both large and small-
the sun that shines to lift the fog
is meant to bless us, one and all!

So, sing *alleluia* to the Lord—
give praise for his magnificent ways.
Our world is filled to overflowing
with blessings to enlighten all our days.

Humanity Unraveled

Our humanity is becoming
unraveled at its very core
driven by speed; quantity reigns
quality is threatened to be no more.

The human voice, the look in the eye
is replaced by waves in the air
when it used to be those very expressions
that would convey a message of loving care.

Can we exist without the hand-written word
sent to touch the human heart?
If voices are unheard, and eyes are unseen
will intimacy fade and become a lost art?

Our ability to communicate
is the glue that keeps us together—
emails and texts can carry our message
yet, the human voice reveals a unique character.

Too much, too fast
without the human touch
can destroy true intimacy
that we humans crave so much.

It's not either-or, one way or the other
where the present overwhelms the past–
it is rather holding on to an intimacy
that builds relationships meant to last.

I want to see the look in your eye,
the very tone of your voice;
I want to receive the hand written note,
kept to cherish–my heartfelt choice.

The Labyrinth Calls, Again

So much like life
with its shadows and light
twists and turns; knowing and unknowing,
consolation and desolation, the path goes on–
Trust the path, my God says to me.
One step at a time; it leads to Me.
Trust even when the path moves away;
it returns–sit and stay awhile.
Trust, you say?
Yes, trust–I am here along the path
to its exit as you re-enter the world.
Trust your path, as the bright yellow flower
proclaims out loud:
"See! I am here blooming
where I have been planted–surrounded by space
lush and green, attractive and pretty, I bloom!"
You have been planted, now bloom!
Walk my path for you–
This is where I am with you,
no place else,
in the nows of your existence
here–now–always!

Behind and Before

I sit in contrast–
Behind me through the glass doors the daily news explodes
in living color and disturbing sound
I am alerted as if I was there–
another bomb–innocence unprotected
evil justified–a blasphemous curse
suspects known yet not apprehended
who, when, where and why
the threat knows no bounds
Before me the black bird soars–
his nest atop the tall oak tree
offers a respite from the coastal breeze.
The horizon stretches the imagination
to limitless unknowing–
the Gulf waters speak in whispers
as the waves gently kiss the shore
and retreat to the company of more–always more.
Such contrasts in the lives of humanity
separated only by a glass door–
we are free to enter or exit
the choice is ours...

The Return of Silence

With a vengeance *She* will return
as the pendulum of our ways
swings from the extremes.
Chaos—noise—busyness
having had its say,
no more can the human heart stand—
constant distractions and
uninvited interruptions lambasting
the tender walls of our forgotten souls.
Finally the bough breaks
and we fall from the incessant rocking
into the Great Solitude.
We find Peace and Comfort
in the everlasting arms of cherished Silence.

When Faith Becomes Personal

When we know that we know that we know;
When words are left unattended;
When rational explanations cannot satisfy;
When the Peace and Joy are overwhelming;
When our world seems brighter
and burdens feel lighter;
When tears have a purpose;
When surrender is a gift;
When the opinions of others have no voice;
When we experience the Holy Presence
within and without;
When our hearts are at rest
no matter the circumstance
and hope rules the day;
When faith becomes personal
we have found the Way.

Unlimited

Just look at the people
created in the Divine Image
no two exactly alike–
even twins having a separate space.
We cover the earth
from pole to pole–
so many possibilities
for Love to shine forth.
The physical is distinctive;
the Spirit is unifying–
How awesome is our God!

Roll Back the Stone

"Come Holy Spirit and roll back the stone
that keeps us from the Light of your Love"–
the stone large and burdensome
keeps us entombed in darkness.
Our minds shrouded in the lies of worry,
a fear that paralyzes Hope...
where new life is in bondage,
doubt and fear "miss the mark"
until with Divine Purpose
a brilliant Light bursts from within–
the stone rolls back–the tomb is empty.
Death is conquered–Love's promise is victorious
Life has a new beginning!

The Other Side of Darkness

Lord, beyond the darkness
your Light does shine
through the valleys
a peaceful reward.
Jesus, you are my Light,
the light of the world.
You are my Shepherd
who guides me through valleys
to mountain top pastures.
You are Lord, Amen and Amen!

Original Goodness of God

The original goodness of God
is victorious over
the original willfulness of "man".
When we said "No, I will go my way"
our omnipotent God knew well
the Son would show the way back
to the Original Goodness of our being.

As Near As

The morning wakeup call
of the unseen yet heard
"Cock-a-doodle-do" of the rooster,
the cooing of the dove–
the sun's rays shining forth
on an awakening dawn–
God is near!
I open my eyes of awareness–
God's presence all around
the early morning breeze
whispers through the awaiting branches
capturing the cardinal's response
to the beginning of yet another day.
God is near!
Leaves flutter with knowing recognition,
the clouds not intended to stay
travel along in surrendered spirit–
God is near!

Alone-ness

The great lie told by the Great Liar:
"It's all up to you; there's no one
to help you; you are on your own."
The lie so great and burdensome
that even in attempts to pray
the Great Truth is hardly heard.
Try as I might; pray as I ought
the darkness prevailed
no end in sight.
Then the Spirit touched
the very heart of me;
a light Spirit enveloped me–
I was among believers,
seekers of Divine Grace–
all was well, all was well!
The grace to trust evades me still
as the thorn of doubt runs ever so deep–
Grace, that prevailing Spirit,
that sufficient supply,
gets me through another day.
I am grateful–all is well, all is well!

Prisons

Not of concrete and steel
but of doubts and fears
enclosing the heart
in a threatening darkness–
a darkness searching
through bars of desolation–
crying out for consolation.
Grace responds:
Jesus, has been in our human prisons
only to break free, a prisoner no longer–
Therein lies our hope!

Paschal Mystery

Aaaaah humankind! You want
light before you experience darkness
joy before pain
healing before suffering
resurrection before death.
Darkness, pain, suffering, death—
doors you must walk through
if you are to experience
light, joy, healing and resurrection.
Jesus, Our Savior, shows us the Way.

A Wakeup Call

The death of a loved one
is a wakeup call for the living–
"Gone" they are,
yet, Faith assures us
with the promise of Hope–
where Love and Eternal Peace
are shared with our God forever.

Coffee with Jesus

When the woman described her moment–
her husband bringing her coffee in bed,
down the treacherous road of envy and self-pity
I was immediately and blindly led–
until I heard the comforting Voice
that rescued me before I completely lost my way:
We have coffee together as part of our
early morning prayer.
don't fret; you are loved and cared for
way beyond compare!
Jesus

Remember When

When I have fallen and can't get up,
remember, I love you;
When my memory fails and I don't
know who I am or what day it is,
remember, I love you;
When I can't recall your name,
don't take it personal,
remember, I love you;
When my needs are great and I am more
and more dependent on your busy lives,
remember, I love you;
When I ask you to repeat your words
much to your patient dismay,
remember, I love you;
Life is such a mystery–
we are given so much
which fades over time
making way for an Eternity
of overwhelming bliss where
there is no loss, only Joy!

Vanity

I am losing my hair,
Vanity whispers her shame;
I have wrinkles and age spots,
Vanity distracts with lies;
My waistline has disappeared,
Vanity knows no limits;
My skin is thinning and easily bruised,
Vanity distorts our wholeness;
My grandchildren call me "old",
Vanity hides their innocence;
"Looks" can kill when that is all there is,
Vanity wins a foolish battle.

Lord, help me to accept the losses of aging. Guard me against the temptations of vanity. Help me to see the gains and relish the Wisdom of seeing as you see—into my heart and soul where true and everlasting beauty resides. Amen!

Midway In-between

We are midway—
in-between the Kingdom of Now
and the Kingdom to Come.
Foretastes of Forever give Hope—
the distance makes no difference
when our Constant Companion
lights our way.

The Ugly Battlefield

Humanity scattered on the
battlefields of life
needs our compassion–
an acknowledged look, an embrace
that goes far beyond our mortal senses.
Entombed in our own needs and desires
we fail the other–yet, the world changes.
Justice surprises our self-centered expectations–
the downhearted and dejected
enter the Kingdom
led by the Shepherd of Compassion–
Who's heart never fails to love.

The Field Hospital

The soldier lies desperate
from the tragedy of war–
the hands of the disciple
are there to comfort him
not to expound on the realities
of a peaceful kingdom yet to come,
but to stop the bleeding
bandage his wounds
thereby offering hope–
the Kingdom becomes real!

Moments of Grace

As diverse as the Creator's love:
the humming bird hoovers;
the cardinal perches;
the mole leaves its tunnel;
the sunflower surprises;
the phone call is timely;
the written word invites reflection;
the seed breaks ground;
the child's smile offers hope;
the laughter brings relief;
the other is forgiven;
the seeing heart rejoices;
another day dawns;
moments of grace abound.
All is well in God's world. Amen

Original Love

God is love:
Through the ages every "yes" to love
has found its origin in our God–
Who is love
Who can only love
Who calls us into being through love
to share that love
the very heart of His kingdom.

Thy Kingdom Come

A smile to a stranger,
Thy kingdom come;
An encouraging word,
Thy kingdom come;
The door held open,
Thy kingdom come;
The last book given,
Thy kingdom come;
"God's will, not mine",
Thy kingdom come;
Time offered,
Thy kingdom come;
Grief shared,
Thy kingdom come;
Laughter uniting,
Thy kingdom come;
Friends and strangers welcomed,
Thy kingdom come;
A hurt forgiven,
Thy kingdom come;
Justice prevailing as mercy is given,
Thy kingdom come;
A fellowship joined in prayer,
Thy kingdom come;
Bread and wine transformed,
Thy kingdom come;
A world saturated with God's love,
Thy kingdom come!

Stress

Calculating, perplexing, and prevailing
you roam our world
like the plague of ancient Egypt
seeking an open portal–
aware we cry out:
*"Lord God, may your Holy Spirit protect me
and relieve me of this burden
for it is too much to carry;
Why have you abandoned me?"*
Surrendered arms let go
and receive a Divine's embrace
All is well.....Amen and Amen!

Saints Among Us

The scientist seeks a cure;
the environmentalist seeks protection;
the "liberal" seeks a new way;
the "conservative" seeks to maintain;
the rebel seeks justice;
the righteous seek truth;
the faithful seek the will of God.
Diversity is creative—
all included for the glory of God!

The Face of God

So many images:
light skin–dark skin
short–tall and all in-between
attractive to the human eye–others not so
physical appearance marvelously diverse–
How do we see the face of God?
Jesus–
gentle and kind;
passionate and forgiving;
generous and compassionate;
obedient to the end of his earthly journey–
qualities not restricted to any one physical form.
His followers giving tribute to his presence among us
like pieces of colorful yarn
drawn toward unity–
The tapestry of the Kingdom is revealed.
His *face* appears.

Heads Bowed

To see my children's heads
bowed in humble prayer
touches this mother's heart
and stirs hope of the Father's care.

Life's not easy with hills and valleys
all along the way,
but our Constant Companion guides us
as we bow our heads and humbly pray.

Trapped But Not Forgotten

(In reference to the 2018 rescue of young
boys from a cave in Thailand)

God was there knowing their every need
sending courageous divers
to seek the seemingly lost;
sending a tenacious Spirit
to strengthen the willing to not give up;
His knowledge had trained the rescue team
to perform His invincible plan—
testing our faith in His power,
He answered unified prayer;
It was the brave hearts and light from within
that the children showed the world;
God was their Light within their cave
as they awaited in hope, not despair.
God's Light did shine in that treacherous labyrinth
that connected the children to safety;
Angels surrounded their tired and weakened bodies
protecting them from harm.
Certainly, there could have been a different ending
to this miraculous tale of human endurance
(and sometimes there is),
but when we find God *in all things*
the mystery of gratitude prevails!

Miracles

A change of heart:
from anxiety to trust;
from bitterness to forgiveness;
from anger to acceptance;
from fear to joy;
from condemnation to understanding;
from darkness to light;
from self to a loving God—Amen!

Unless

The groaning of early morning traffic
gives birth to a day just begun
and deafens the human ear to the songs
of early morning greeters rejoicing
in the gift of sunrise.
The unheard noise of random thoughts rush about
like thistles scattered in the wind of unrest
crowding the day's possibilities.
Anxiety blinds the human eye to the
vivid color of early Spring
as unexpected flowers grow along the roadside
beneath a sky painted in yet unidentified hues.
A fast gulp of reliant caffeine
gives us that anticipated jolt
leaving its taste on a hospitable pallet–
preoccupation with the demands of the
day's deadlines always looming
suffocates the smell of the ginger, the scent of the rose
or rain soaked earth.
Physical touch, whether a hug or a hand
vanishes into a schedule of measured time–
UNLESS
We slow down, relax in order to rejoice and receive
all that makes us human
formed in the image of our Creator–
Seeing, hearing, tasting, smelling, touching, feeling.
Oh God, how great Thou (we) art!

What's Your It?

Without the struggles and challenges of *addiction,*
I would not have the direction of recovering
friends who support me;
Without a *divorce*
I would not have been brought to the
"bottom" needed to grow
mentally, emotionally, and spiritually
by focusing on my own faults
instead of on the faults of others;
Without the *death of my spouse*
I would not know the graces of solitude and how
loss becomes a blessing– how faith and hope
promote a reunion beyond the grave;
Without the *pain and suffering of my loved ones*
I would not be learning the power of intercessory prayer
to trust in God's unconditional love and provision;
Without *It* all
I would not be who I am today or be on the path that I am on,
uniquely mine, for the glory of a merciful God.
Embrace your *it* for *it* all belongs!

Holy Nudges

Let's go for a walk
Make that phone call
Visit your neighbor
Wash those dishes
Time to be still
Read that passage
Receive the Eucharist
Work in your garden
Admit your wrongs
Forgive your offenders
Take the risk
Attend the meeting
Answer the phone call.
Holy nudges I send to you—
Divine invitations for your day.
Trust my nudges,
God

Courtship Feeding

From my kitchen window I could see
the male cardinal attentively feeding
the female perched nearby–
feeling like I was eavesdropping
on an intimate, private exchange.
Information so readily available
describes this ritual as "courtship feeding"–
Nature having her way and teaching us once again
like the cardinal
our God courts us each and every day
in hopes of a more surrendered intimacy.

A Mother's Prayer

It seems there comes a time in a mother's life
when all that is left for her "to do" is "to be"
in surrendered prayer.
Gone are the opportunities to set down
and enforce rules in order to guide and protect–
now in the "letting go" time
trust draws her deeper into the heart of Faith,
that place of the unseen
where God is at work behind the scenes
and He is not sharing His secrets.

Wisdom reveals itself through awareness
of God's Presence through generations of intercessory prayer–
from mother to mother to mother
prayers offered holding no judgment or condemnation
only hope and a deep level of surrender.
Many a child has come to know God
through the loving prayers of her/his mother.

The Walk

They walked at the edge of the road
a pair to catch the noticing eye–
she carried a small grocery bag
a knapsack hunkered on the back of the child
his short legs competing for success
as he labored to keep pace.
How far had they walked?
How much further did they have to go?
Did they not have a car, or someone to drive them?
With downcast eyes she made her way
careful of every step and the need to protect the child.
So many others driving by–to and fro, to and fro
a circumstance taken for granted by most–
teaching lessons of a simpler more humble life
where God makes his presence known
despite seeming hardship.
Perhaps some would be moved to pity
missing the inner strength it takes for her
to walk her walk,
an inner strength that questions me–
Would I be able to do the same?

Jesus, the Way—the Truth—the Life

He came to show us how to love
and we crucified him with hate;
He came to show us how to forgive
and we opted for vengeance;
He came to show us the Father
and we accused him of blasphemy;
He came to give us the Kingdom
and we chose the familiar.
The choice continues–
May we choose his way, his truth, and his life
for therein lies the Kingdom.

Limitless Love

Love's power to endure is beyond measure—
a truth declared from times of old
reminding us that agony and pain
make way for love to unfold.

For, as Jesus hung on the cross
he was left quite alone
his disciples had abandoned him
scattered in fear, no faithfulness shown.

It was his mother along with a few
who witnessed his last breath.
We, too, can find her comfort
now and at the hour of our death.
Amen!

Called to Prayer

The call to prayer is pure gift–
a time for Light to shine on
early morning darkness;
a time to calm the storms
of worry and anxiety;
a time to hear words of
hope and peace;
a time when faith is renewed for
yet another day;
a time to praise God from whom
all blessings flow;
a time for gratitude–
*Thank you God for this day
and all it will bring. Amen*

Listen

The song of the bird
invites me to stop, be still, listen—
a heavenly chorus of notes
drifting through unoccupied space.
Who taught this bird to sing
such a sweet melody
sung in resolute efforts
to praise his Creator?
Who indeed!
Heaven must be filled to overflowing
with such never ending praise, *Alleluia!*

From Major to Minor

Children require a lot of energy
as they pass through their early years—
decisions made for them
despite resistance and tears.

Parents play a *major* role
in guiding those in their care—
it's not yet the season of complete surrender
when into God's hands we leave them there.

So, from major to *minor*
our roles gracefully transform—
releasing them into God's hands
becomes our prayerful norm.

Just About Money

When it's not just about money
we are free to follow our dreams;
When it's not just about money
the *children's hour* has its place;
When it's not just about money
politics is set aside letting conscience be our guide;
When it's not just about money
we are good stewards and reverence Nature's bounty;
When it's not just about money
we spend valued time in the service of others;
When it's not just about money
we experience peace beyond our understanding–
A peace that proclaims, "All is well in God's world"
and it's not just about money. Amen!

Out of Grace

Like a fish out of water
stranded from the water's edge
I struggle to survive.
I flip and flop gasping for the intended life of grace,
experience having taught me to be patient–
the sustaining waves will return surrounding me
to carry me home.

Amen and Amen!

Amen! So be it for the glory of God
and the good of our soul;
the coffee is made,
Amen;
the dishwasher is loaded,
Amen;
a "good morning" is shared,
Amen;
the groceries are shelved and forgotten,
Amen;
the clothes are folded,
Amen;
the floors are cleaned,
Amen;
a neighbor is visited,
Amen;
a listening ear is given,
Amen;
a piece of art is created/words written,
Amen;
a new path taken,
Amen
prayer fills the silence,
Amen;
a routine is followed and broken,

Amen;

the garden is weeded and planted,

Amen;

a meal is prepared,

Amen;

forgiveness is requested and given,

Amen;

acceptance of what is,

Amen;

Jesus is Lord,

Amen;

Prayer in all things,

Amen and Amen!

CPSIA information can be obtained
at www.ICGtesting.com
Printed in the USA
FSHW011507311020
75326FS